PENGUIN DREAMS
AND STRANGER THINGS

Bloom County Books by Berke Breathed

BLOOM COUNTY BABYLON –
Five Years of Basic Naughtiness
BILLY AND THE BOINGERS
TALES TOO TICKLISH TO TELL
PENGUIN DREAMS and Stranger Things

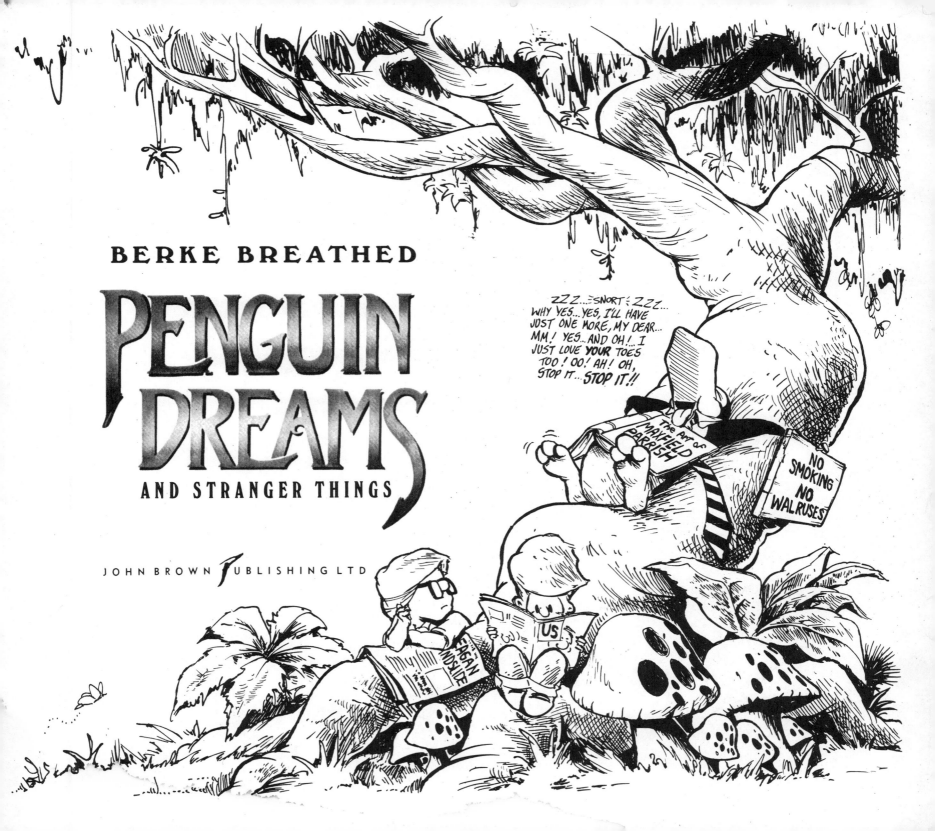

FIRST U.K. EDITION 1989
BLOOM COUNTY IS SYNDICATED BY THE WASHINGTON POST WRITERS GROUP
FIRST PUBLISHED IN THE U.S. AND CANADA BY LITTLE, BROWN & COMPANY
ISBN 1 870870 08 5

PRINTED IN SPAIN

MILO'S ALBUM

A Personal Photographic Statement

A self portrait. Behind is
the boarding house. Steve
Dallas' room is in the back.
(250 at f 16)

A private moment. Steve
Dallas sings Julio Iglesias.
I was under the bed.

The USS Starchair
"Enterpoop" slips into Warp
Drive. Mr. Spock watches
for "The Wild Planet of
Open-minded Stewardesses"

Oliver Wendell Jones disciplines a
reluctant Banana Junior Computer,
apparently eager to catch "2010"
at the Bijou

*Binkley finally confronts his neuroses
in the only appropriate manner.*

November 5, 1984...
A gallant sense of optimism
prevails in the face of
impending, overwhelming
stomach-churning
political catastrophe.

"But the calculations were
Correct!"
The scientific pursuit of the
first long-tailed hamster
is dealt yet another serious
blow.

7:13 a.m., Sunday morning.
"Quality Time"

WELL...I MUST SAY...THIS CRUISE HASN'T EXACTLY BEEN WHAT I EXPECTED. AT LEAST I CAN LOOK FORWARD TO A GOOD GOURMET DIN—...

UH...WHAT'S THIS?

BEAN CURD AND SHREDDED WHEAT.

OH. ACTUALLY I WAS HOPING FOR A NICE BIG STEAK...

MEAT?!?

NO?...UH...WELL, I LOVE SHREDDED WHEAT, TOO! YES...YES, I'LL JUST EAT SCRUMPTIOUS SHREDDED WHEAT. NO PROBLEM.

ANY SUGAR?

REFINED SUGAR?!?

EXCUSE ME, FELLOW SHIPMATES...BUT I WONDER IF YOU MIGHT EXPLAIN JUST WHAT THE DICKENS IS GOING ON AROUND HERE...

THIS CRUISE SEEMS TO BE NOTHING BUT A BUNCH OF BEAN CURD NIBBLERS WALKING AROUND TALKING TO WHALES AND PLANNING "CONFRONTATIONS" WITH NUKE WASTE DUMPERS. NOW, JUST WHAT IS ALL...

UH... ALL...

...GOOD HEAVENS!... OF COURSE! WHY,...YOU ALL ARE... ARE...

ENVIRONMENTAL EXTREMISTS.!!

NO! YES!

T WAS THE DAY BEFORE CHRISTMAS, AND FAR OUT AT SEA, A PENGUIN WAS SEARCHING FOR HIS MOM, PATIENTLY.

FOR, YOU SEE, ONE CAN MANAGE GROUNDHOG DAY WITHOUT HOGS... BUT A CHRISTMAS LESS MOTHERS IS STRICTLY FOR THE DOGS!

RAINBOW WARRIOR

SO WHILE WE ALL SIT, IN OUR HOMES COMFORTABLY, WITH FAMILY ABOUT, CHUGGING EGGNOG AND TEA...

RAINBOW WARRIOR

...LET'S REMEMBER ALL THOSE ON TOMORROW'S BRIGHT DAWN, WHO'LL BE CUDDLING THEIR NOSE, IN PLACE OF A MOM...

YEAH!

13

AND SO, HOME. AND WITH AN UNSUCCESSFUL CONCLUSION TO THE ANTARCTIC "MOMQUEST"... THE MOOD JUST ISN'T VERY GOOD...

PHPHPT!

..HIJACKED BY "GREENPEACE"... HARPOONED BY RUSSIAN WHALERS, INVOLUNTARILY RESCUED BY U.S. MARINES...

PHPHPT!

YES, IT IS TIMES LIKE THESE WHEN IT IS BEST FOR ALL CONCERNED THAT WE BECOME JUST ONE VERY SPECIAL THING...

...ALONE.

PHPHPT!

MY LIFE NEEDS SPIRITUALITY. YEP. THAT'S IT. I NEED RELIGION.

BUT WHICH ONE? I MEAN, THERE'S A LOT RIDING ON THIS.

CHECKED THE "YELLOW PAGES"?

OH, IT'S A CONSUMER'S NIGHTMARE. TOO MANY BRAND NAMES.

I WOULDN'T TAKE ANY CHANCES.

I'M JOINING 'EM ALL.

GOOD EVENING. TODAY'S TOP STORY: GIANT RADIOACTIVE SALAMANDERS ARE MOVING UP FROM MEXICO AND DEVOURING ALL PUDGY, FLIGHTLESS WATERFOWL.

YOU'RE KIDDING!

WE'RE NOT KIDDING.

YOU HAVE TO BE KIDDING!

WE'RE NOT KIDDING.

OH MY GOODNESS... OH MY GOODNESS... YOU'VE GOTTA BE KIDDING!!

WELL, WE'RE KIDDING A LITTLE.

THE MEDIA'S GETTING COCKY!

19

WHO IS IT?! WHO'S BANGING ON THE DOOR OF MY ANXIETY CLO- SET-?!!

CRAZED CONSUMERS! LET US IN!!

NO! CHRISTMAS IS OVER! NOW GO AWAY AND ACT LIKE CIVILIZED HUMAN BEINGS!!

LET US IN! WE KNOW THEY'RE IN THERE!

AAARGH!

LADY, THERE ARE NO "CABBAGE PATCH DOLLS" IN HERE--

I'VE GOT ONE!!

GOOD EVENING. THIS IS ABC WORLD NEWS TONIGHT. TODAY, NOTHING HAPPENED.

TONIGHT ON AN EXTENDED "NIGHTLINE", TED KOPPEL WILL GET TO THE BOTTOM OF THIS LACK OF NEWS.

THIS SUNDAY ON "THIS WEEK WITH DAVID BRINKLEY", GEORGE WILL AND SAM DONALDSON WILL ARGUE ABOUT ALL THIS NOTHING.

AND LATER TONIGHT WE'LL HAVE A SPECIAL ABC CLOSE-UP... "NOTHING : IS IT SOMETHING?" GOODNIGHT!

YOU, UH, EXPECTIN' COMBAT?

"SURVIVALISM", BOY. STEVE DALLAS IS SHOWIN' ME HOW TO BE A "SURVIVALIST"...

THE WORLD'S DISINTEGRATING, SON...THEY'RE GONNA DROP THE BIG ONE ANY DAY NOW... AND THERE'LL BE ONLY A FEW OF US TO SURVIVE PAST THOSE FIRST FEW STEPS OUT OF OUR CUSTOM BUILT BOMB SHELTERS...

...AND THOSE WILL BE THE STRONG...THE BRUTAL...YES, THE SAVAGE...BITING... MAIMING...CLAWING... KILLING TO SURVIVE!! AND THAT'LL BE ME... ME!!

WELL. IT'S NICE TO SEE YOU KEYED UP ABOUT SOMETHING...

YEAH. GOD, I COULD EAT A TREE.

HERE, APPARENTLY, ARE A PAIR OF EXPERT "SURVIVALISTS" ON THEIR WAY TO DIG A BOMB SHELTER IN THE MEADOW... SAY, BOYS, ANY TIPS FOR US AMATEURS?...

NO NO... RUSH! RUSH! NO TIME TO CHAT...

WHAT ABOUT FOOD? WHAT DO EXPERT SURVIVALISTS PLAN TO EAT AFTER THE "BIG ONE" DROPS?

EAT? WELL,...AS I UNDER-STAND IT, WE'LL BE HUNTIN'... MAYBE A LITTLE 'COON... 'POSSUM...SOME RABBIT...

POING!

NOW JUST WAIT ONE ☆◎!!?# MINUTE...

DID YA GET ALL THE SUPPLIES?

YESSIR! K-MART WAS OPEN LATE.

LESSEE... 9MM AMMO...WATER PURIFIERS...GAS MASKS... FALLOUT SUITS...RADIATION SICKNESS PILLS...RADIOACTIVITY DETECTORS... UH...

AWRIGHT. HOLD IT...

WHERE'S THE MUTANT REPELLENT?

AW SHOOT...

LET'S SEE, NOW... "CONDUCT A SURVIVALIST DRILL," HE SAID..."THE BOMBS HAVE DROPPED AND YOUR DUTY IS TO DEFEND THE RADIOACTIVE RUBBLE OF THE MIDWEST AGAINST THE ENEMY..."

"...AND ALL YOU'VE GOT IS YOUR GUN...WHICH IS LIKE A MISTRESS; TREAT HER WITH RESPECT AND SHE'LL NEVER POOP OUT ON YOU."

"SO GRASP HER RESPECTFULLY... SIGHT ENEMY... AND SLOWLY SQUEE —"

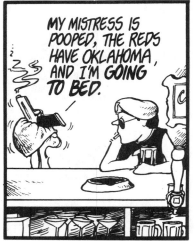

MY MISTRESS IS POOPED, THE REDS HAVE OKLAHOMA, AND I'M GOING TO BED.

YES... WELL, I'M CERTAINLY VERY HAPPY THAT YOU WERE ABLE TO BUY THE BLOOM COUNTY TELEPHONE CO., MR. POODINSKI...

THANKS TO THE FEDS!

YEP! NOTHIN' LIKE A COMPETITIVE MARKET TO KEEP THE CUSTOMERS HAPPY!

UH... SPEAKING OF CUSTOMERS... I WONDER IF I COULD GET A NEW EXTENSION PHONE INSTALLED?

NO SWEAT! WHAT'S A GOOD DAY FOR YA?

UH... TUESDAY.

FINE. HOW'S JULY OF '86?

BARTENDER! I'LL HAVE A CUP OF COFFEE! STRAIGHT UP!

COFFEE LETS YOU CALM YOURSELF DOWN WHILE IT PICKS YOU UP! AND I'M ONE OF THE NEW COFFEE GENERATION!... ONE OF TODAY'S MOVERS AND SHAKERS! YESSIR... I'VE JOINED THE COFFEE ACHIEVERS!!

OR IS IT ALL JUST A BUNCH OF HOOEY?

GOOD MORNING, DAD. I BROUGHT YOU SOME MILK AND DOUGHNUTS. YOU'LL NEED THE NOURISHMENT FOR THE TASK AHEAD.

BELOVED FATHER OF MINE... I CAN NOW ANNOUNCE THAT EVERY ONE OF YOUR CIGARETTES HAS BEEN SECURELY HIDDEN. AS WELL AS YOUR CAR KEYS. IN SHORT, THIS WEEKEND WILL BE SPENT SANS TOBACCO.

HAVING SAID THAT, LET'S BEGIN THERAPY. READY?

HERE, OF COURSE, IS AN ENLARGEMENT OF A DISEASED LUNG. IN COLOR.

PTEWPH!

THAT'S IT, SON. YOU WIN. I GIVE UP. I'VE TOTALLY AND SHAMEFULLY DEGRADED AND HUMILIATED MYSELF.

SO, NO MORE SMOKING. NOPE! NEVER AGAIN. I'LL PROMISE...

IF...UH...IF YOU'LL JUST TELL ME ONE SILLY, NAGGING, LITTLE THING...

JUST WHERE THE **HECK** DID YOU HIDE MY CIGARET——

TOILET.

I'VE BEEN ASKED BY THE MANAGEMENT TO ANNOUNCE THAT, STARTING TODAY, YET ANOTHER NEWSPAPER WILL BE PRINTING THIS FEATURE...NAMELY, THE **TULSA DAILY HERALD.** SO FAR, THAT MAKES A TOTAL OF SIX NATIONWIDE. OBVIOUSLY, WE'RE VERY EXCITED.

BLOOM TOURS

SO, TO HELP OUR NEW VIEWERS IN TULSA, I THOUGHT IT'D BE NICE TO SPEND THE NEXT FEW WEEKS CONDUCTING A BASIC INTRODUCTORY TOUR OF BLOOM COUNTY.

BLOOM TOURS

YES...WELL...NOW THEN... WE CAN START RIGHT HERE. WE'RE STANDING IN "MILO'S MEADOW." OVER THERE IS "BINKLEY." TO MY LEFT HERE IS "PORTNOY.".

BLOOM TOURS

AND ME? I'M "MICHAEL JACKSON."

MY FANNY.

BLOOM TOURS

AND NOW, FOR THE BENEFIT OF ALL OUR NEW READERS IN TULSA, LET'S FIRST VISIT THE GRAVESITE OF BLOOM COUNTY'S MOST FAMOUS AND HIGHLY RESPECTED FORMER RESIDENT... **BILL THE CAT.** HE WAS — HEY! WHAT'S **THIS**?!

BLOOM TOURS

AHOY, MAN! STOP THAT! WOULD YOU SO EASILY TREAD UPON THE HOLY RESTING PLACE OF LINCOLN? OR KENNEDY? OR ELVIS?!

ZZZ... SNORT!

BILL 1980-1983

SHOO! SCRAM! AWAY WITH YOU, YOU DISRESPECTFUL SCALAWAG!

WAP! WAP! WAP!

I'M SO EMBARRASSED! BILL THE CAT IS CONSIDERED A NEAR-DEITY BY EVERYONE! TRULY!

POINK! POINK! POINK!

29

30

WAKE UP, STEVE, WAKE UP! YOU'VE WON A ROLE IN *TESS TURBO'S* NEW VIDEO AND THE CAMERA CREW IS ON ITS WAY OVER!!

QUICK! WE NEED TO GET YOU DRESSED! OO...YA KNOW, THESE ROCK VIDEOS GET PRETTY WILD...WE'LL NEED TO FIND SOMETHING APPROPRIATE...

LESSEE...SOMETHING SHOCKING...CRAZY... TACKY...OUTRAGEOUSLY UGLY...

PERFECT! EL BARFO!

THAT'S MY SUNDAY SUIT!!

ONCE MORE... I'M GONNA BE IN A ROCK VIDEO WITH **WHO**?

"TESS TURBO." SHE'S ON HER WAY OVER HERE IN HER TOUR BUS AT THIS VERY MOMENT.

WHO'S TESS TURBO?

ROCK STAR. HEAVY METAL. HERE'S A PHOTO.

I READ IN "ROLLING STONE" THAT SHE'S REALLY A VERY SWEET, SENSITIVE GIRL IN REAL LIFE...

ZZZ... SNORT... ...SCUZBALL ~YA AIN'T NOTHIN' BUT A SCUZZZZZ... HMPH... SNORT

HELLO, MR. DALLAS! WE'RE HERE!

ESTHER NUBERGER... TESS TURBO'S MANAGER. VERY, VERY GLAD TO MEET YOU, STEVE!

OH, THIS SHOULD BE FUN... VIDEOS ALWAYS ARE! NOW WHILE THE FILM CREW SETS UP, YOU JUST LET US KNOW IF THERE'S ANYTHING WE CAN DO FOR YOU...

..ANYTHING AT ALL.

THANKS. YA KNOW, THEY SHOOT PEOPLE LIKE YOU WHERE I COME FROM.

34

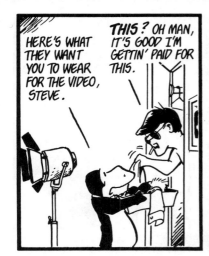

HELLO. I'M MS. GAIL SMITH... THE HOSPITAL'S PSYCHOLOGICAL COUNSELOR. I'M HERE TO HELP YOU BECOME SOCIALLY AND SEX- UALLY ACCEPTED INTO SOCIETY AS A NEW QUADRUPLE AMPUTEE.

AMPUTEE?!

HOLD IT. AREN'T YOU MR. BUD DAVIS?

NO. I'M MR. STEVE DALLAS AND I'VE HAD ALL MY CHEST HAIR PERMANENTLY FRIED OFF.

OH MY.

SO. HOW SHOULD I DEAL WITH THIS?

YA GOT ME. SMOOTH-CHESTED MEN LEAVE ME CLAMMY.

HELLO, NURSE. I'M DR. OPUS. I'D LIKE TO PRESCRIBE SOME SPECIAL MEDICATION FOR MR. DALLAS DOWN THERE IN ROOM 316...

LESSEE... "A 20 oz. SIRLOIN STEAK, STUFFED ARTICHOKES, SAUTEED BELGIUM MUSHROOMS, STRAWBERRY CREPES, SEVERAL LIMES, A CASE OF TEQUILA, AND AN AFFECTIONATE, SWEDISH MASSEUSE."

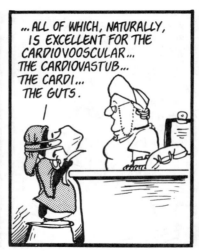

...ALL OF WHICH, NATURALLY, IS EXCELLENT FOR THE CARDIOVOOSCULAR... THE CARDIOVASTUB... THE CARDI... THE GUTS.

SHE'S NOT BUYING IT!!

SECURITY PLEASE...

AND NOW LET'S MEET THE LITIGANTS AS THEY ENTER THE COURTROOM...

HERE'S THE PLAINTIFF, MR. STEVE DALLAS, WHO SAYS THAT WHILE FILMING A ROCK VIDEO WITH THE DEFENDANT, A SPECIAL- EFFECTS BLAST IGNITED HIS CHEST HAIR... HE'S SUING FOR $10 MILLION.

AND HERE'S THE DEFENDANT, MISS TESS TURBO, WHO SAYS THAT THE PLAINTIFF DESERVED EVERYTHING HE GOT SINCE HE'S A COMPLETE JERKFACE. SO NOW, JOIN US TODAY ON "THE PEOPLE'S COURT."...

...FOR "THE CASE OF THE CHARRED- CHESTED CHUMP."

WATCH YOUR MOUTH.

PLAINTIFF

38

SO THE CASE OF "THE CHARRED-CHESTED CHUMP" COMES TO AN END. AND HERE COMES THE PLAINTIFF NOW...

MR. DALLAS...YOU LOST YOUR CASE, JUDGE WAPNER YELLED AT YOU, AND YOU'VE BEEN HUMILIATED IN FRONT OF MILLIONS OF PEOPLE... WHAT DO YOU HAVE TO SAY?

I DON'T FEEL LIKE TALKING ABOUT IT.

JUDGE WAPNER CALLED YOU A *24-KARAT IGNORAMUS"... I WONDER IF —

YA KNOW, MY ALL-TIME FAVORITE SONG IS "YESTERDAY." WHENEVER I HEAR IT, I THINK OF FROLICKING PORPOISES UNDER ANTARCTIC RAINBOWS. I DUNNO WHY... IT'S JUST A VERY SENTIMENTAL SONG TO ME...

THEY FINALLY MADE A VIDEO FOR IT. I SAW IT THIS MORNING. IT WAS MOSTLY SLOW-MOTION EXPLOSIONS AND HALF-NAKED WOMEN SLINKIN' AROUND.

WOULD YOU LIKE TO KNOW WHAT I THINK OF NOW WHEN I HEAR "YESTERDAY"?

HALF-NAKED, EXPLODING PORPOISES!

OH MY...

TO COMPUTE... OR NOT TO COMPUTE... THAT IS THE QUESTION...

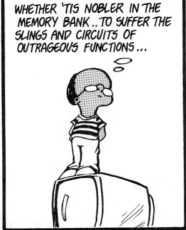

WHETHER 'TIS NOBLER IN THE MEMORY BANK .. TO SUFFER THE SLINGS AND CIRCUITS OF OUTRAGEOUS FUNCTIONS ...

.. OR TO TAKE UP ARMS AGAINST A SEA OF...TRANSISTORS. OR RATHER, TRANSPONDERS... TRANSCONDU- TRANS... ER...

OH, TO HACK WITH IT.

...IN HONOR OF WHAT WOULD HAVE BEEN BILL THE CAT'S FOURTH BIRTHDAY, VARIOUS CHARTER MEMBERS OF THE NATIONAL BILL THE CAT FAN CLUB HAVE BEEN ASKED TO SHARE THEIR FEELINGS ON TODAY'S BITTERSWEET OCCASION:

OO...BILL HOWLED THE SONGS WHICH MAKE THE WHOLE WORLD SING...OO, BILL HOWLED THE SONGS AND SAID STUUUPID THINGS...OO, BILL HOWLED THE SONGS WHICH MAKE THE YOUNG GIRLS SICK...YES, BILL IS GROSS BUCKETS!... AND HE HOWLS THE SONGS!...

YEAH!

COOKIN' NOW!

OO! OO! OO!

HELLO, THIS IS MY OWN CAT "ELVIS SNOOGUMS." I LOVE CATS. ELVIS IS 9½. I FORCE-FEED HIM PETROLEUM JELLY FOR HIS HAIRBALLS. IF HE CROAKS, I'LL NAME THE NEW ONE "BILL SNOOGUMS."

BILL IS SIMPLY A VUNDERFUL FELLOW. A GOOD FRIEND...GOOD BACKGROUND...AND OO!... IS BUCKLEY LOADED! LOTSA DOUGH! AND I TINK DAT...UH..DAT... HUH? VHAT? VHAT'S WRONG? ISN'T ALL DIS FOR "BILL DA ARISTOCRAT?"

I LOVED BILL THE CAT. SO I MADE THIS BILL DOLL OUT OF SOME OLD CURTAINS. I THINK IT IS A GOOD LIKENESS. MOM WANTS TO BURN IT 'CAUSE IT MAKES THE DOG THROW UP.

AH YES...BILL THE CAT...GOOD OL' BILL THE CAT... GOOD OL' DUMB STUPID UGLY HAIRY SMELLY BILL THE ★⊃#!! CAT...MMPHMPH!

CREEAK...

AND SO IT STARTS AGAIN... MIDNIGHT MONSTERS AND NOCTURNAL NASTIES...ONE CAN ONLY WONDER WHAT OTHER FOLKS FIND IN THEIR LATE-NIGHT ANXIETY CLOSETS...

STEVE DALLAS...ON BEHALF OF ALL YOUR PAST LOVERS...I'D LIKE YOU TO KNOW THAT WE ALL THINK THAT WHEN IT COMES TO KISSING, YOU RANK ALL THE WAY UP THERE WITH... WELL ... WITH SQUID.

HA HA HA HA HA

OLIVER WENDELL JONES!... I AM THE GHOST OF SLIDE RULES PAST...COME BACK TO ME!!

AAIGH! NEVER!!

GREETINGS, MR. BLOOM. WE'RE DA COPY-RIGHT LAWYERS FER UNITED FEATURE SYNDICATE. ME AND ROCCO BEEN NOTICIN' A FEW SIMILARITIES TWIXT OUR "GARFIELD" AND DAT "BILL DA CAT" JOIK... AIN'T DAT RIGHT, ROCCO?

YEAH... RIGHT...

YOU, UH... WHITE MEAT OR DARK MEAT?

SMACK

WELL, MR. BINKLEY...YOUR SON'S APTITUDE TESTS SEEM TO INDI-CATE THAT HE'S BEST SUITED FOR DESIGNING LADIES' EVENING WEAR. OR COLLECTING GARBAGE. EITHER ONE.

AN EDITORIAL REBUTTAL

The publishers of this feature welcome Professor Burton Wellsly Kingfish III, Dean of the Harvard School of Law, with his presentation of an opposing viewpoint to opinions previously and innocently expressed in this space.

50

I'M SORRY, MA... I'M NOT STAYING IN TO WATCH TV WITH YOU TONIGHT. NOT TONIGHT. NO WAY. TONIGHT I GO OUT!

AND I REFUSE TO FEEL GUILTY ABOUT IT! IN FACT, I PLAN TO ACT IRRESPONSIBLE, GET DRUNK, COMMIT CRIMES AGAINST NATURE AND GET DANGEROUSLY MIXED UP WITH THE KIND OF WOMEN YOU IMAGINE ME WITH IN YOUR WORST NIGHTMARES!

OKAY!... HERE I GO! SEE YA LATER, MA! HERE I GO!

"FAMILY FEUD" OR "TIC-TAC-DOUGH." YOU CHOOSE.

DO YOU SMELL THAT, OPUS? DO YOU SENSE WHAT'S IN THE AIR THESE DAYS?

Milo's Meadow

SPRING?

NO... MORE THAN THAT... IT'S IN THE WIND... BREATHE DEEP... WHAT DO YOU SMELL?

SNORT SNORT

SNIFF!

M. Mead...

DIRTY SOCKS.

POLITICS!

M. Mea...

IT'S CAUCUS TIME!!

AND SO IT WAS. INDEED, IT WAS TIME TO REIGNITE THE SLUMBERING FIRES OF POLITICAL FERVOR AMONG THE MEADOW PARTY FAITHFUL...

I'M FERVOROUS! I'M FERVOROUS!

WAP! WAP!

...AND TO REINVIGORATE THE PREVIOUSLY NOMINATED VICE-PRESIDENTIAL CANDIDATE...

YOUR WAKE-UP CALL, MR. OPUS...

YES, IT PROMISED TO BE A TIME TO REMEMBER!

A RAUCOUS CAUCUS, AS IT WERE.

BOBBLE BOBBLE BOBBLE BOBBLE

HERE'S THE SCHEDULE OF THE SPECIAL-INTEREST GROUPS THAT OUR VICE-PRESIDENTIAL CANDIDATE WILL BE VISITING THIS WEEK. THAT'S YOU.

I AM AWARE OF THAT.

LESSEE... MONDAY IS THE "BROTHERHOOD OF STAMMERING WORM FARMERS"... TUESDAY, "BOSTONIANS FOR BUDDHA"... WEDNESDAY, "THE GAY SPELUNKER'S ASSOCIATION."...

AND OF COURSE, THURSDAY IS PHYLLIS SCHLAFLY'S CIVIL RESTRICTIONS GROUP... THE "L.A.W.".

WHAT'S THAT?

"LADIES AGAINST WOMEN"

OO... SOUNDS RADICAL.

AND THUS DID THE CANDIDATE TAKE HIS SPECIAL CAMPAIGN MESSAGE TO THE PEOPLE...

THE PEOPLE

...A MESSAGE OF HOPE... OF DELIVERANCE... OF UNIVERSAL JOY:

AHEM...

NO MORE "WHERE'S THE BEEF?" JOKES!!

POUND!

AND THE PEOPLE REJOICED!

GOD BLESS YOU, BROTHER!

YES, YES... THANK YOU! HALLELUJAH!

AHEM...

GRBLB BLABT UNT MIPT SPEEB!! OOT PIFFOO BLABOO...

WOULD SOMEONE PLEASE GIVE THE TELEPROMPTER A SWIFT KICK...

52

AND I SAY THAT THIS COUNTRY IS ONCE MORE HUNGRY FOR MEN OF PEACE... MEN OF LOVE... AND I AM THAT CANDIDATE...

PPHPPTH!

..A CANDIDATE OF COMPASSION... OF TOLERANCE... OF SIMPLE, HUMAN TENDER——

PPHPPT! PHFFPT!!

STICK THAT SLOBBERING TONGUE OUT ONCE MORE AND I SHALL SLICE IT OFF AND FEED IT TO THE TURTLES!!

I HATE HECKLERS.

GREAT SPEECH. PPHPFT!

NOW, BEFORE WE GET DOWN TO CAUCUS BUSINESS, HODGE-PODGE WOULD LIKE TO LEAD US IN A PRAYER.

LORD, BLESS OUR LITTLE GROUP AND BOTH TYPES OF FOLKS WHO ARE IN IT...

THE AMERICAN MEADOW PARTY

"THE LONG-EARED" AND "THE SHORT-EARED..."

THE AMERICAN MEADOW PARTY

OR RATHER, "THE LONG-EARED" AND "THE UNWASHED HEATHEN."

JUST A MINUTE...

THE AMERICAN MEADOW PARTY

WHAT SHORT-EARED, UNWASHED INFIDEL INTERRUPTS OUR INSTITUTIONAL PRAYER?

ME! I DON'T LIKE PRAYERS FOR LONG-EARED FOLKS!

THE AMERICAN MEADOW PARTY

WELL I'M LONG-EARED AND I'M DOIN' THE PRAYIN' SO YOU JUST LISTEN!

POO! NOT WITH MY SHORT EARS!

EXCUSE ME.

THE AMERICAN MEADOW PARTY

I'M AFRAID I DON'T HAVE ANY EARS WHATSOEVER.

THE AMERICAN MEADOW PARTY

YOU CAN SIT OUT IN THE HALL.

RATS.

THE AMERICAN MEADOW PARTY

AND THUS THE VOTES WERE VOTED AND THE DELEGATES DELEGATED... AND, BY GOLLY, THE PRESIDENTIAL NOMINATION APPEARED ALL LOCKED UP...

OH NO... OH NO NO NO...

YES, THE PEOPLE HAD SPOKEN.. AND THEY HAD SAID...

BILL THE CAT!!

...WHICH PRESENTED THE SEASON'S FIRST POLITICAL CRISIS.

HE'S DEAD!!

POUND!

YEAH, WELL, SO WAS GARY HART.

AND NOW! AVAILABLE AT LAST! THE IBM 4000 PC SR SYSTEM... BUT NOW FEATURING TINT CONTROL!

HACKERS, AS A RULE, DO NOT HANDLE OBSOLESCENCE WELL.

OLIVER WENDELL JONES! I HAVE SOMETHING FOR YOU!

COMING, MOTHER.

HERE.

A GLOVE?

A MICHAEL JACKSON GLOVE! FOR MY OWN LITTLE MICHAEL JACKSON!

WELL. THAT'S VERY CONSIDERATE OF YOU. YES. A "MICHAEL JACKSON GLOVE," YOU SAY?

LIKE IT?

I'M IN PARADISE. WHERE'S THE OTHER ONE?

SO! I UNDERSTAND YOUR MOTHER'S BEEN WORKING ALL DAY TO TURN YOU INTO "HER OWN LITTLE MICHAEL JACKSON", EH, SON?

TRAGICALLY, IT IS TRUE.

WELL, YA LOOK TERRIFIC! BOY, SHE DIDN'T MISS A DETAIL, DID SHE? NOPE! NOT A SINGLE... UH...

SON... WHERE'Z THE REST OF YOUR EYEBROWS?

FLOATING IN THE HALL TOILET.

THAT BIG CLOUD LOOKS LIKE A FLUFFY CASTLE TO ME. WHAT'S IT LOOK LIKE TO YOU, OLIVER?

A LARGE, CUMULUS CLOUD.

OH, THAT'S GREAT. A TYPICALLY COLD, SCIENTIFIC RESPONSE. YA KNOW, IT'S THAT VERY SAME LACK OF SOUL WHICH ALLOWS BRAINY TYPES SUCH AS YOURSELF TO GROW UP AND CREATE SCIENCE WITHOUT CONSCIENCE...LIKE **THE ATOM BOMB!**

SO TURN OFF THE CALCULATOR, OLIVER, AND TURN ON THE SOUL!!

NOW, WHAT'S THAT CLOUD LOOK LIKE?

AN ATOM BOMB.

SAY, BINKLEY... WHAT'S THAT CLOUD LOOK LIKE TO YOU?

ME? OH. WELL. LESSEE... IT LOOKS LIKE... A BIG FACE. WITH A DOUBLE CHIN. AND BIG TEETH.

WHAT'S IT LOOK LIKE TO YOU?

RAIN.

PAD PAD PAD

HELLO! YES OH **YES** I'D LIKE TO TAKE ADVANTAGE OF YOUR ONCE·IN·A·LIFETIME SPECIAL TV OFFER FOR THE AMAZING RONCO COMBINATION "PLUM PITTER AND YOGURT SQUIRTER"... FOR ONLY $39.98!!

IT DICES! IT SLICES! IT SHPLICES! IT PUSHES! IT MOOSHES! IT SQOOSHES! TRULY A DREAM MACHINE! DON'T FORGET THE FREE BONUS "POCKET DIAPER STEAMER!" I'LL TAKE SIX THOUSAND!! THANK YOU! GOOD-BYE!!

AWRIGHT... THAT'S IT. NO MORE LATE-NIGHT TV FOR YOU.

YES... YES, THAT'D PROBABLY BE FOR THE BEST...

I GOT SIX THOUSAND RONCO COMBINATION "PLUM PITTER AND YOGURT SQUIRTERS" FOR A MR. OPUS.

SORRY. THERE'S NO "OPUS" HERE.

RONCO

RONCO

YEAH DERE IS. SEZ RIGHT HERE... "MR. OPUS, 533 SUMMIT STREE—"

HE DIED. LAST WEEK. HIT BY A BLIMP.

RONCO

WELL WHAT DA ★@!!# AM I S'POSED TO DO WI--

SORRY. THANK YOU. GOOD DAY.

RONCO

HE'S GONE.

OH, I AM **SO** EMBARRASSED!

NO WAY. WE HARDLY KNOW EACH OTHER. BUG OFF.

C'MON, PRETTY LADY... DON'T BE COY...

NO. I'M SORRY, BUT "THE SEXUAL REVOLUTION" IS OVER.

WHAT? SINCE WHEN?

I'M NOT SURE. LAST MONTH, I THINK. "TIME" MAGAZINE SAID SO.

BIG SHMEAL!

CARING... IS BACK "IN."

I CARE FOR YOU, HOT MAMA!!

57

CANDY! SWEETCAKES! WHERE YA GOIN'?

I...I DUNNO. I'M JUST GOING.

LISTEN.. I'VE GOT A BOTTLE OF '66 CHÂTEAU LAFITE OVER AT MY PLACE. LET'S..!..

NO, STEVE. "TIME" SAID THE SEXUAL REVOLUTION IS OVER. THINGS CAN'T BE THE SAME ANYMORE.

BABY... LISTEN TO ME... IT'S A HOAX... A VICIOUS MEDIA RUMOR... A MEAN, TERRIBLE, AWFUL, NIGHTMARISH --

STEVE...

WHAT?

I'D LIKE TO GO HOME AND PUT ON A PETTICOAT.

WILL SOMEONE PLEASE TELL ME JUST WHAT IN BLUE BLAZES IS GOIN' ON WITH THE WOMEN IN THIS BAR?!

Ladies Night TUESDAY ½ PRICE C

YEAH! WHAT'S WITH THE CHICKS?

WHAT'S ALL THIS BUSINESS ABOUT "CARING" AND "EMOTIONAL COMMITMENT"?!

I CAN'T DEAL WITH EMOTIONAL COMMITMENT! I'M A SWINGING, HEDONISTIC BACHELOR!

...I'LL TELL YA WHAT IT IS! IT'S "TRADITIONAL AMERICAN VALUES" CREEPING BACK IN!!

NOW?!! BUT I JUST GOT MY HAIR IMPLANTS!

MY GOD. WE'VE GOT TO GET CARTER BACK IN THE WHITE HOUSE.

ALAS.. THE SCENE AT "BOB'S BAR AND FLESH MARKET" SIMPLY WASN'T VERY PRETTY...

I AM RUINED.

..DRIED-OUT HULKS OF FRUSTRATED BACHELORHOOD LAY ROTTING ON THE SINGLES BEACH OF LIFE AS THE TIDE OF THE SEXUAL REVOLUTION QUICKLY RECEDES...

SIGH...

..TRAGIC REFUGEES...ALONE IN THE COLD, CELIBATE WINTER OF THE '80s..

DOESN'T...DOESN'T ANYBODY WANT TO SHARE MY PERSONAL SPACE TONIGHT?

YES, AN ERA WAS OVER. AND NONE WERE TO SUFFER MORE THAN THE SEXY AND FORMERLY ACTIVE MEMBERS OF THE OFFICIAL "BLOOM COUNTY STUD SQUAD"...

WELL! THIS IS A FINE HOW-DO-YOU-DO!

YEAH!

I...I CAN'T TAKE TAKE ANOTHER NIGHT OF "TRIVIAL PURSUIT."

60

MADAM, YOU'VE BEEN CHOSEN TO BE THE FIRST TO WITNESS THE WORLD'S ONLY GENETICALLY ENGINEERED, **LONG-TAILED HAMSTER.** FOLLOW ME.

AAIGH!

YES... YES, IT'S AN EMOTIONAL MOMENT FOR ME AS WELL.

TH...**THAT'S YOUR** "LONG-TAILED HAMSTER"?!

"SUCCESS" IS RARELY TOTAL IN SCIENCE. TRY TO SEE THE FOREST FOR THE TREES, MOTHER.

AAAIGH!!

THIS IS A TAIL.

TONIGHT, WE'LL BE SHOWING YOU ALL HOW TO PREPARE EVERYONE'S FAVORITE SUMMER DISH: "ROAST PENGUIN RUMP."...

.. SERVED WITH DELICIOUS JELLIED PENGUIN TONGUE...

AND GARNISHED WITH YUMMY PENGUIN NIBLETS!

"YUMMY **WHAT?**"

DON'T ASK.

AND THERE IT IS! HOT AND READY TO SERVE... "ROAST PENGUIN WITH RAISINS." LET'S GET SOMEONE FROM THE STUDIO AUDIENCE TO GIVE IT A TASTE!

HERE YA GO, MA'AM... AND HAVE SOME GRAVY... DIG IN AND TELL US WHAT YA THINK...

A LITTLE FATTY.

TRY A LEG.

I THINK THAT'S QUITE ENOUGH, THANK YOU.

HELLO, MRS. WHACKER. I'M YOUR LAWYER, STEVE DALLAS. PLEASE EXCUSE MY APPEARANCE... I'M SUFFERING FROM AN AWESOME HANGOV-- ER...HEADACHE.

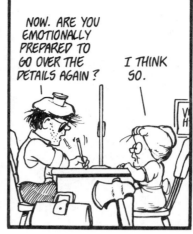

NOW THEN...DON'T YOU WORRY... NO ONE REALLY BELIEVES YOU AXE-MURDERED YOUR HUSBAND. LEAVE MATTERS TO ME AND I'LL GET YOU OUT OF THIS MESS. NO PROBLEM.

NOW. ARE YOU EMOTIONALLY PREPARED TO GO OVER THE DETAILS AGAIN?

I THINK SO.

WHAT WERE YOU DOING AT THE TIME OF THE ALLEGED CRIME?

ALLEGEDLY TURNING CHARLIE INTO CHOPPED LIVER! WHACKITY-WHACK!

NOW, MRS. WHACKER... YOU **KNOW** YOU DIDN'T MURDER YOUR HUSBAND... YOU'RE JUST UPSET... CONFUSED...

NOW YOU JUST LISTEN TO ME...

FOR TEN YEARS, CHARLIE HAD BEEN HANGING HIS DIRTY SOCKS ON THE HALL BANISTER, SPITTING ON MY GERANIUMS, AND CALLING ME "PUDGE-POT." AND LATELY HE'D BEEN FORCING ME TO WATCH "DICK CLARK'S CENSORED BLOOPERS" EVERY DAMNED FRIDAY NIGHT...

NOW I ASK YOU, MISTER DALLAS... WHAT WOULD **YOU** DO IF YOU WERE MARRIED TO SUCH A MAN?

WELL --

YOU'D TAKE AN AXE TO 'IM, THAT'S WHAT YOU'D DO!

AND NATURALLY YOU'D LIKE YOUR CLIENT FREED WITHOUT BAIL BECAUSE SHE ISN'T ACTUALLY A HOMICIDAL AXE MURDERER.

SHE'S A LAMB, YER HONOR.

WELL, FINE, MR. DALLAS! SHE'S RELEASED INTO YOUR CARE UNTIL THE TRIAL.

MY CARE?

SPECIFICALLY... YOUR **HOUSE**.

MY HOUSE?

GOOD DAY. OR RATHER, GOOD-BYE.

NOW WAIT A MINUTE...

WOOSH!

63

YEP. THAT'S IT. ALL THROUGH.

THE EFFICIENT LEGAL SECRETARY TO FAMED ATTORNEY STEVE DALLAS HAS FINISHED THE DAY'S WORK AND IS SETTLING INTO BOREDOM.

IT IS IDLE TIME SUCH AS THIS WHEN THE GREAT AMERICAN OFFICE WORKER KNOWS **EXACTLY** WHAT TO DO...

...XEROX VARIOUS PARTS OF ONE'S BODY WHEN NOBODY'S LOOKIN'.

EL BLOB! GET IN HERE!

COMING, YOUR LEGALNESS!

TAKE A LOOK AT WHAT I FOUND IN THE WASTEBASKET. SOMEBODY'S BEEN MESSING WITH THE XEROX MACHINE. CAN YOU MAKE OUT JUST WHAT THE HECK THIS IS A COPY OF?

WELL, LET'S SEE...

IT COULD BE A LOAF OF BREAD. OR SEVERAL POUNDS OF COOKIE DOUGH. OR A DEFLATED VOLLEYBALL. VERY DIFFICULT TO SAY, EXACTLY.

IT MIGHT ALSO BE AN **EXTREMELY** ATTRACTIVE TUCKUS.

WAKE UP! WAKE UP! TODAY'S THE DAY! HALLELUJAH, HOT PATTOOTIES! IT'S **TRIAL** DAY!!

YES, BOLDLY, THE HOT, YOUNG DEFENSE ATTORNEY PREPARES FOR THE FIRST BLOODY BATTLE... BUT **FIRST**... A DRESS REHEARSAL FOR THE OBLIGATORY PRESS CONFERENCE ON THE COURTHOUSE STEPS...

THE VIDEOTAPES ARE RIGGED! THE WITNESSES ARE CORRUPT! THE PROSECUTORS ARE NAZI DRUNKARDS AND MY CLIENT WAS FRAMED! BY THE WAY, SHE WAS BORN-AGAIN LAST TUESDAY. AND I HAVE NO FURTHER COMMENT SINCE I CERTAINLY WOULDN'T WANT TO SEE THIS CASE TRIED IN THE MEDIA.

YET ANOTHER TRIUMPHANT PERFORMANCE OF THE FAMED "DELOREAN DESPERATION DEFENSE"!

GOOD MORNING AND WELCOME TO THE LIVE COVERAGE OF THE BLOOM COUNTY AXE MURDER TRIAL... BROUGHT TO YOU BY *CNN*, THE NETWORK WHICH BROUGHT YOU THE NEW BEDFORD GANG RAPE TRIAL.

LIVE 8:06 A.M.

AS WE PAN ACROSS THE ROOM, WE SEE THE DEFENSE COUNSEL, APPARENTLY GOING OVER LAST MINUTE STRATEGY.

STEVE? YOO HOO!

AND HERE, OF COURSE, IS THE DEFENDANT, MRS. ALICE "ONE-STROKE" WHACKER, ACCUSED OF TURNING HER HUSBAND INTO LIVERWURST.

BILL LIVES

BUT NOW, A WORD FROM OUR SPONSOR...

GINSU CUTLERY

YOUR HONOR, BEFORE WE START THIS SHINDIG, THE DEFENSE MOVES TO HAVE ALL THE CHARGES AGAINST MY CLIENT DISMISSED. MY ASSISTANT WILL NOW CITE THE RELEVANT CASE PRECEDENT.

AHEM. "THORSON VS. LIBERACE," 1982. A 23-YEAR-OLD MAN FILES $113 MILLION PALIMONY SUIT, CLAIMING EMOTIONAL AND SEXUAL DEPRIVATION AFTER THE FAMED PIANO PLAYER FAILED IN HIS PROMISE TO... GET THIS... *ADOPT* HIM.

VERY NICE.

THANK YOU.

AND TOTALLY IRRELEVANT.

OH, BUT IT CERTAINLY IS A WONDER!

YER HONOR, THE PROSECUTION WOULD LIKE TO SUBMIT THE FOLLOWING EVIDEN—

I OBJECT!

I OBJECT TO THAT MOTION! I OBJECT TO YOUR NOSE! I OBJECT TO CRUMMY TV MINI-SERIES! I OBJECT TO THE ARMS RACE! AND I OBJECT TO CHRONIC HUNGER IN A WORLD OF PLENTY!!

I OBJECT! I OBJECT! I OBJECT! I OBJECT! BY GOLLY, I OBJECT!

BAM! BAM! BAM! BAM!

DAMN THE TORPEDOES! GO FOR THE GUSTO! BITE THE BIG ONE!... *THAT'S* WHAT I ALWAYS SAY!!

WE INTERRUPT FOR A DRAMATIC DEVELOPMENT AT THE AXE MURDER TRIAL. THE DEFENDANT HAS APPARENTLY FOUND A PLASTIC PICNIC KNIFE AND IS NOW RUNNING AMOK IN THE COURTROOM.

HERE'S JUDGE KIRBY, NO DOUBT CALMLY INSTRUCTING THE JURY NOT TO ALLOW THEMSELVES TO BE PREJUDICED BY THE PRESENT ACTIVITIES.

AND THIS APPEARS TO BE THE UNDERSIDE OF A TABLE. WE'RE GETTING REPORTS THAT THE DEFENDANT IS TRYING TO FILLET OUR CAMERAMAN...

OOPS. THAT'S IT. BACK TO ATLANTA.

..WE, THE JURY, FIND THE DEFENDANT, NOT GUILTY.

WHAT?

THAT'S RIGHT! NOT EVEN A SMIDGEN GUILTY!

ARE YOU PEOPLE ORANGUTANS? ANYBODY CAN SEE THAT WOMAN IS A MENACE!

BUT WE LADIES HAVE CERTAIN INSTINCTS.

SO DO I. SHE'S GUILTY... SHE HAS TO BE.

LOOK, YOUNGBUNS, GUILTY AXE MURDERESSES SIMPLY DON'T WEAR "GEORGIO ARMANI."

BUT THEY DO SELL MOVIE RIGHTS!!

O SOOTHING SUN, ON SUMMER WINGS... MAKES ME FORGET SO MANY THINGS!

LIKE WAR AND HATE AND BASIC BADNESS, LIKE FEAR AND PAIN AND LONELY SADNESS...

BUT MOST OF ALL FOR GOODNESS SAKES...

I FORGET MY PARKING BRAKES.

BINKLEY, I'D LIKE TO HAVE A LITTLE TALK.

MY PLEASURE.

SON, YOUR MOTHER AND I HAVE BEEN DIVORCED FOR A WHOLE YEAR NOW...FOR ME, A LONG, **LONELY** YEAR. AND NOW, LIFE MUST GO ON.

I THINK IT'S GETTING VERY CLOSE TO THE TIME WHEN SOMEONE NEW WILL BE ENTERING OUR LITTLE NEST. A NEW FACE...A NEW SMILE... A NEW LIFE TO LOVE AND HUG AND KISS.

SON, DO YOU REALIZE WHAT I'M TRYING TO SAY?

YOU'RE PREGNANT.

HELLO, MOM? THIS IS YOUR SON. I THOUGHT YOU MIGHT LIKE TO KNOW THAT, LATELY, YOUR EX-HUSBAND HAS GONE OFF THE MORAL DEEP END.

HE'S PACING AROUND LIKE A STARVING PUPPY...SAYING HE NEEDS "THE COMFORT OF A WOMAN'S CARESS.. THE WARMTH OF HER LIPS...AND THE TINGLING TOUCH OF HER FINGERTIPS."

NOW SURELY DAD WASN'T WALLOWING IN THIS SORT OF MORAL SEWER WHEN **YOU** WERE STILL HERE, WAS HE, MOM?

GRIEVOUSLY, TRAGICALLY, UNFORTUNATELY, NO.

WELL, I DIDN'T THINK— HOW'S THAT?

SON...I...I'D LIKE TO GO OUT ON MY FIRST DATE. HOW DO YOU FEEL ABOUT THAT?

I'M NOT SURE. MORE IMPORTANTLY, HOW DO **YOU** FEEL ABOUT IT?

WELL, I THINK I'M READY. I'VE WAITED A LONG TIME. AND I **HAVE** MATURED.

THAT YOU HAVE. I RECKON MY LITTLE DIVORCÉ IS ALL GROWN UP!

THEN YOU DON'T OBJECT?

GET OUTTA HERE, COWBOY!

GOSH! THANKS, SON!

TAKE THE CAR. HERE'S A FEW BUCKS...

SON... I'M BRINGING MY DATE IN... FOR JUST A SECOND... SO PLEASE TRY... TRY NOT TO SAY ANYTHI—

OH, TINY HINEY! HERE COMES MAMA!

HA! HA! SHE'S... UH, SHE'S SURE A REAL KIDDER!

WAAEELL... WHAT A FAHN LOOKIN' LITTLE RUG RAT!

HI, BABYCAKES... I'M "STORMEE" WITH TWO "E"s.

I'M "APPALLED" WITH TWO "P"s.

MY GOODNESS, WHY JUST LOOK AT THE TIME!...

WELL. SHE CERTAINLY IS SOMETHING, DAD.

ISN'T SHE, THO?

...:THE MOMENT I FIRST SAW HER IN THE K-MART HARDWARE DEPT., I SAID, "WHOA! NOW THERE'S A SENSITIVE GAL WITH GOOD LOOKS, TO BOOT!"

YA KNOW... I'VE NEVER ASKED WHAT SHE DOES. WHADDYA THINK SHE'S INTO, SON?

GOBS OF HICKEYS WITH "DURAN DURAN."

COME AGAIN?

I HAVE A SURPRISE FOR YOU, OLIVER. I WALLPAPERED YOUR ROOM, TODAY!

WALLPAPER! IN MY LABORATORY? IN MY PRIVATE THINK TANK?!

I PICKED THE DESIGN MYSELF! GO LOOK!

FEARLESSLY, THE MALE OFFSPRING STRIDES TOWARD WHAT MUST SURELY BE A TRULY GARGANTUAN, AESTHETIC CATASTROPHE... PINK CHOO-CHOO TRAINS? STRIPED BLIMPS? THE MIND BOGGLES!

GOOD HEAVENS.

WHY DID I PUT MICHAEL JACKSON WALLPAPER ON YOUR WALL?...WELL, I'D BE HAPPY TO TELL YOU WHY...

..BECAUSE MICHAEL DOESN'T SMOKE, DRINK, TAKE DRUGS, CURSE OR FOOL WITH LOOSE WOMEN, THAT'S WHY.

DARN IT, OLIVER, YOU MIXED-UP KIDS COULD **USE** A GOOD, HEALTHY, ROLE MODEL, THESE DAYS!

MOTHER, THE MAN'S BEST FRIEND IS A BOA CONSTRICTOR NAMED "MUSCLES".

OLIVER WENDELL JONES? ARE YOU THERE, DEAR?

KNOCK! KNOCK!

DEAR, YOU HAVEN'T YET TOLD YOUR EASILY INSULTED MOTHER JUST HOW MUCH YOU **LOVE** YOUR NEW MICHAEL JACKSON WALLPAPER. DEAR?...

PRIVATE

OH, OOOOLIVERRR ...?

WELL, I MUST TELL YOU THAT I AM PLEASED **NOT A BIT** WITH THE LOCATION OF NEXT MONTH'S MEADOW CONVENTION.

SAN FRANCISCO IS NICE IN SUMMER!

CALIFORNIA IS STOCKED WITH CRAZY PEOPLE, DEAR BOY. WOULD YOU LIKE TO KNOW WHAT THE LATEST, HONEST TO GOODNESS **FAD** IS OUT THERE?

NO.

WELL, I'LL TELL YA ...

NOT INT'RESTED.

FIREWALKING.

HEY, I VOTED FOR DES MOINES!

73

74

WELCOME, DELEGATES, TO THE 1984 NATIONAL MEADOW CONVENTION. OKAY...SETTLE DOWN...I HAVE AN ANNOUNCEMENT.

CBS, NBC AND ABC HAVE ALL DECLINED TO COVER THE PROCEEDINGS. IN FACT, APPARENTLY NOBODY REMEMBERED TO INFORM THE PRESS THAT WE EVEN EXIST.

HOWEVER.. MTV IS HERE. AND AS I UNDERSTAND IT, THEY'LL BE BROADCASTING OUR CONVENTION LIVE AND PUTTING IT ALL TO THE MUSIC OF...UH... — WHO IS IT?

"JUDAS PRIEST."

YES. AND ALL DUE TO THE EFFORTS OF OUR EX-PRESS SECRETARY, MICHAEL "SUSHI-FOR-BRAINS" BINKLEY.

WHY, HELLO, MILO. HOW ARE THINGS AT THE CON-VENTION?

I'M NOT SURE, OLIVER. GO TURN ON MTV AND TELL ME HOW WE'RE COMING ACROSS TO AMERICA.

UH.. I SEE A SHOT OF OPUS GIVING A SPEECH. BUT THEY'RE PLAYING HEAVY METAL ROCK MUSIC OVER THE PICTURE.

YOU'RE NOT GETTING ANY OF THE SPEECH? GO TURN IT UP AND TELL ME WHAT YOU HEAR.

"DRAG ME THROUGH THE HELL-SLIME, MAMA, SATAN--"

: CLICK! :

THANK YOU, TENNESSEE. THAT'S 87 VOTES FOR BILL THE CAT. MAY WE HEAR FROM THE TEXAS DELEGATION?

YEEE HAW!

FROM THE GREAT PECOS RIVER IN THE WEST TO THE MIGHTY HERDS OF LONGHORNS IN THE EAST, ACROSS THE DUSTY PAN-HANDLE TO THE WINDY SHORES OF THE SOUTH...

TEXANS FOR BILL THE CAT

TEXAS

...WE GOT 126 HIGH-TOOTIN' VOTES FOR THE NEXT CHIEF COWPOKE OF TEXAS AND THESE OTHER, LESSER UNITED STATES... BILL THE CAT!!

HYAH!

HYAH!

THANK YOU. AND LET'S KEEP THE REGIONALISTIC EMOTIONALISMS UNDER OUR BIG, UGLY HATS, SHALL WE?

CAREFUL, BOY.. I WOULDN'T GO A-PUTTIN' NO PRICKLY BURRS UP MY TAILPIPE, IF YA GETS MAH DRIFT, YA LITTLE PRAIRIE POOP.

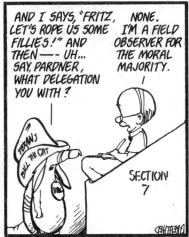

"BILL'S DRAMATIC RETURN" —SEQUENCE #2—TRANSITION SHOT~HOLD ''' AND ZOOM IN SLOW FOR IDENTIFICATION—

KEEP ZOOMING ~AUDIENCE IS BEGGING INFORMATION~ KEEP ON EDGE OF SEATS WITH VISUAL FIREWORKS —CLOSE IN ~

TIGHT SHOT ~SOFT FOCUS— FAMILIAR FEATURES BECOME VISIBLE—KEEP ZOOMING TIGHTER ''' TIGHTER—

TOO MUCH !! MOOD RUINED! FACE-LIFT SCARS VISIBLE RESHOOT

"BILL'S DRAMATIC RETURN" SCENE #3~"SPIELBERG SHOT" ~LOW ANGLE ~WIDE LENS FRONT LIT FOR EFFECT— SUBJECTS REACT TO SIGHT OF CAT ~

—REVERSE SHOT—LOW + WIDE '' 3/4 VIEW—GLYCERIN ON TONGUE FOR GLISTENING EFFECT—HOLD

REUNION ~DRAMATIC CRANE SHOT—PULL BACK + UP FOR EMOTIONAL CLIMAX —HIGHER ''' HIGHER '''

TOO HIGH !! AND TOO DAMNED SILLY! SCRATCH WHOLE EPISODE! START FRESH MONDAY!

WELCOME BACK, SON! I'VE BEEN COOKING YOU A SURPRISE...

YOU'VE HAD WOMEN IN THE HOUSE WHILE I'VE BEEN GONE, HAVEN'T YOU, DAD?

UH-HUH! UH-HUH! I LEAVE FOR JUST ONE WEEK AND THE HAPPY HOME BECOMES AN UGLY NEST OF IRRESPONSIBLE DIVORCÉ BEHAVIOR...

I CAN SMELL THE CHEAP PERFUME...ADMIT IT... YOU'VE BEEN MESSING WITH WOMEN OF QUESTIONABLE MORAL CHARACTER.

SNIFF!

NO, I'VE BEEN MESSING WITH TARTS.

NARY A DIFFERENCE!

"THE OLD MAN HAS HAD A DAME STAYING IN THE HOUSE DURING MY ABSENCE," THOUGHT THE YOUNG AND SUSPICIOUS SON, RECENTLY BACK FROM A LONG TRIP...

"BUT THEN LET'S NOT JUMP TO CONCLUSIONS," THE BOY QUICKLY THOUGHT... PRIDING HIMSELF ON HIS BASIC FAIRNESS...

... THERE WASN'T, AFTER ALL, ANY EVIDENCE TO SUPPORT SUCH AN IDEA.

OF COURSE, HE HADN'T YET FOUND THAT CAN OF "NAIR" SITTING ON HIS TUB LOOKING REMARKABLY LIKE SHAMPOO.

NBC! THE PLACE TO BE FOR ELECTION YEAR COVERAGE... FEATURING OUR EXCLUSIVE NBC COMPUTERIZED POLL RESULTS!

HACKERS ONLY

WARDROBE

STAY OUT

HIDE THE WENCHES AND BATTEN DOWN THE ACCESS CODES... YER ABOUT TO BE BOARDED, YE SCURVY NETWORK NEWS DOGS! HAR HAR...

Enter: "NBCNEWS"

BEEP! CLICK!

≡BEEP!≡ PASSWORD INCORRECT. ENTRY INTO NBC NEWS FILES NOT APPROVED.

BEEP! BEEP!

Enter: "DAN RATHER IS A TURNIP."

≡BEEP!≡ APPROVED.

THE DUDE IS HOT!

FRAZZLED
THE UGLY, SORDID LIFE, DEATH
AND REBIRTH OF BILL THE CAT

EXCLUSIVE

THIS WEEK'S
SERIALIZED
INSTALLMENT:
"The Fall of
a Giant"

BOB WOODWARD

SUNDAY. SEPTEMBER 9, 1983...THE COMICS PAGE OF THE L.A. HERALD EXAMINER. WEDGED BETWEEN "HI AND LOIS" AND "ZIGGY", A LIMP CAT LIES NEARLY COMATOSE. BILL HAD CHOSEN THE METHOD MOST POPULAR AMONG TODAY'S SUPERSTARS TO DEAL WITH SPECTACULAR SUCCESS: HE MELTED HIS BRAIN.

HMMMPH! SNIFF! SNORT!

THE SAME DAY. WASHINGTON. THE SENATE/COMICS GUILD HEARINGS...

IT'S ALL A MEDIA MYTH, SENATOR. THERE IS NO MORE A DRUG PROBLEM IN THE CARTOON INDUSTRY THAN IN...OH...SAY, THE ENTERTAINMENT INDUSTRY.

WELL! THAT IS A RELIEF!

LATER, SOURCES CLOSE TO BILL WOULD ANONYMOUSLY RECOUNT THE GREAT CAT'S FINAL, SAD DAYS.

ONE DAY HE STARTED CHASING THE GIRLS AROUND THE POOL WITH A PAIR OF ICE TONGS, SCREAMING "PIRANHA!" — HE WAS CLEARLY OUT OF CONTROL. THEN HE TOSSED ONE OF THE SWANS INTO THE JACUZZI. HEF NEVER LET BILL INTO THE MANSION AGAIN.

ONE NIGHT BILL SHOWED UP ABOUT 4:00 A.M. AT MY WEST HOLLYWOOD BUNGALOW. HE WAS WHACKED. A MOVIE DEAL JUST FELL THROUGH AND HE WAS UPSET, SO HE THREW A CINDER BLOCK THROUGH THE WINDSHIELD OF MY NEW BMW 533. THEN HE DRANK ALL MY ROOT BEER, STOLE MY MERCEDES AND RAN OVER MY MITT. I NEVER SAW HIM ALIVE AGAIN. I'M VERY DEPRESSED ABOUT THIS.

ALL I KNOW IS THAT RIGHT BEFORE HE WAS KILLED, HE TOLD ME THAT HE BELIEVED HE WOULD COME BACK IN HIS SECOND LIFE AS SHIRLEY MacLAINE. YEP!... THE DRUGS HAD CLEARLY TAKEN THEIR TOLL. AND DON'T USE MY NAME WITH THIS!

NEXT WEEK... "THE FINAL 24 HOURS"

FRAZZLED
THE UGLY, SORDID LIFE, DEATH
AND REBIRTH OF BILL THE CAT

EXCLUSIVE

THIS WEEK'S
SERIALIZED
INSTALLMENT:
"THE LAST
24 HOURS"

BOB WOODWARD

TUESDAY. SEPTEMBER 30TH. 7:16 A.M. A LATE-NIGHT PARTY IN COMIC STAR MARY WORTH'S LOS ANGELES HOME. BIG NAMES. BIG MONEY. BIG TEMPTATIONS... BIG SINS. IT FINALLY BREAKS UP WITH THE DAWN. "NEED A LIFT HOME?" ASKS SNUFFY SMITH. HE'S NOTICED BILL, WHO LOOKS BAD. "ACK," REPLIES THE CAT AND STUMBLES TOWARD HIS CAR. SMITH SHRUGS.

11:05 A.M. ROUTE 66. EAST TOWARD HOME. BILL'S NERVOUS SYSTEM—RAVAGED BY MONTHS OF CHEMICAL ABUSE—TEETERS PRECARIOUSLY ON THE BRINK OF TOTAL, CATASTROPHIC FAILURE...

SNORT!

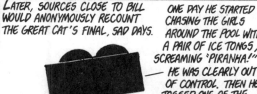

HIGH NOON. THE OUTSKIRTS OF BLOOM COUNTY. 143 M.P.H. OBLIVION... DEAD AHEAD...THE PIPER IS ABOUT TO BE PAID...

VROOOM!! VROOOM!!

CACTUS AHEAD

SCREEEEEECH!

BILL

7:43 P.M. A SCENE OF TOTAL AUTOMOTIVE DEVASTATION. A LONE AND SORROWFUL FIGURE DISCOVERS THAT OF THE ONCE GLORIOUS BILL THE CAT...NOT ONE SCRAP REMAINS. NOT ONE SINGLE, SOLITARY PIECE... EXCEPT...

GREAT SCOTT! IT'S HIS...HIS...

NEXT WEEK: THE SHOCKING SECRET

FRAZZLED

THE UGLY, SORDID LIFE, DEATH AND REBIRTH OF BILL THE CAT

BOB WOODWARD

STILL EXCLUSIVE

The Third and Hopefully Final Installment: "He Hath Risen Again"

IT WAS MILO BLOOM, FRIEND AND BUSINESS ASSOCIATE OF BILL THE CAT, WHO FIRST ARRIVED AT THE SCENE OF THE FIERY CAR CRASH. IT WAS ALSO HE WHO DISCOVERED THE ONLY INTACT PORTION OF THE ONCE GREAT ENTERTAINER WHICH REMAINED...HIS **TONGUE**.

HOW TOTALLY GROSS.

≡SNIFF!≡ HERE...TAKE IT, OLIVER WENDELL JONES....≡SOB!≡ I'M...I'M TOO STRICKEN WITH GRIEF...THIS IS ALL THAT'S LEFT OF BILL...PLEASE...GIVE HIM A NICE BURIAL OR SOMETHING...

OR SOMETHING.

Milo's Meat Wagon

...OR SOMETHING, INDEED! FOR THERE WERE STILL LIVING **GENETIC THINGUMAJIGS** AND DNA **DOOHICKEYS** IN THAT OL' TONGUE OF BILL'S! AND THUS BEGAN THE MOST DARING EXPERIMENT EVER TO BE CONDUCTED BEFORE BEDTIME... THE CLONING OF A CAT!

ACK!

Junior Chemistry

THERE WERE, QUITE NATURALLY, SOME MINOR SETBACKS...

DRAT!

BUT THEN, SUCCESS! AND WHILE OLIVER W. JONES—SCIENTIST, HACKER AND MICHAEL JACKSON DETRACTOR—SLEPT EXHAUSTED, AN UNKNOWING WORLD MOURNED A SOUL WHO HAD FILLED THE LIVES OF MILLIONS WITH HOPE, JOY AND CAT SPITTLE...A SOUL WHO HAD ALSO...**RETURNED!**

ACK YECH BARF SNORT

SON? BINKLEY! I'M TURNING IN NOW. EVERYTHING FINE?

WELL, NO, ACTUALLY... MY CLOSET OF ANXIETIES HAS JUST DISGORGED A WHOLE GAGGLE OF GREMLINS.

THEY'RE ALL ROMPING ABOUT MY ROOM AND CAUSING A GREAT DEAL OF FUSS. WORSE, THEY ALL LOOK VAGUELY FAMILIAR. IN FACT, THERE'S A GREMLIN WHICH LOOKS FRIGHTENINGLY SIMILAR TO WALTER MONDALE AND HE'S SWATTING MY BEHIND WITH A COPY OF JIMMY CARTER'S MEMOIRS.

THAT'S WONDERFUL, SON. NONE OF IT MAKES ONE BIT OF SENSE. YOU'RE A NINCOMPOOP. NOW GO TO SLEEP.

KIDS. WHAT THEY NEED IS A GOOD DOSE OF REALITY.

PARENTS. WHAT THEY NEED IS A GOOD DOSE OF FREUD.

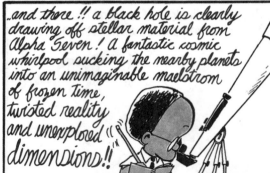

WE INTERRUPT THIS PROGRAM FOR A SPECIAL MESSAGE FROM THE UNITED STATES FEDERAL ELECTION COMMISSION...

ON OCTOBER 28TH, THE AMERICAN MEADOW PARTY BROADCAST A PAID POLITICAL COMMERCIAL NARRATED BY THEIR V.P. CANDIDATE SHOWN HERE.

THE COMMERCIAL INCLUDED TWO PHOTOGRAPHS APPARENTLY SHOWING RONALD REAGAN AND WALTER MONDALE IN CLOSE ASSOCIATION WITH FIDEL CASTRO AND MADALYN MURRAY O'HAIR, RESPECTIVELY.

THE COMMISSION HAS LEARNED THAT THE PHOTOS HAD BEEN TAMPERED WITH.

THEM! THEY MADE ME DO IT! MY ADVISORS! THEM! THEM! THEM!

THE FOLLOWING ARE THE GENUINE, UN-DOCTORED PHOTOS WHICH CLEARLY SHOW WHO THE CANDIDATES WERE ACTUALLY APPEARING WITH...

"BULLWINKLE..."

AND "PUGSLEY" FROM "THE ADDAMS FAMILY".

WE HOPE THOSE RESPONSIBLE FULLY REALIZE JUST EXACTLY HOW MUCH TROUBLE THEY'RE IN.

OH, THEY DO, MAN, THEY DO!

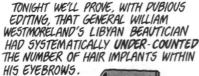

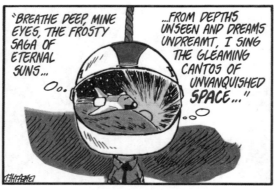

AND NOW, HERE'S ROGER MUDD WITH THE COMPUTER RESULTS FROM THE LATEST NBC NEWS POLL...

THANKS, TOM. WE ASKED AMERICANS IF THEY THOUGHT GERALDINE FERRARO WOULD ATTRACT VOTERS TO THE DEMO- CRATIC TICKET. ACCORDING TO THE COMPUTER, 83% REPLIED, "BASSET HOUNDS GOT LONG EARS."

"BASSET HOUNDS GOT LONG EARS"?

RIGHT. AND THE OTHER 17% SAID, "HOLD THE PICKLES."

IT WAS ALL I COULD THINK OF.

THIS MEANS SOMETHING, ROGER.

AND NOW HERE'S ROGER MUDD WITH COMPUTER RESULTS FROM ANOTHER NBC NEWS POLL.

TOM, WE POLLED 4,000 REPUBLI- CANS REGARDING AUTO AIR BAG LEGISLATION. ACCORDING TO THE COMPUTER, 74% FELT THAT "OODLES OF GREEN NOODLES MAKE BLUE POODLES JUMP DER SHTROODLE."

WHAT?

THAT'S WHAT IT SAYS: 74%, NOODLES, POODLES AND SHTROODLE.

MY FINEST FREE VERSE!

DRUG HUMOR IS IN BAD TASTE, ROGER.

YOU READ IT, TOM!

PORTRAIT OF A SMALL HUMAN... A DIMINUTIVE HOUSE-APE OF THE SPECIES "BINKLEY".

PORTRAIT OF A CLOSET... CHOCK FULL OF ADOLESCENT ANXIETIES AND ASSORTED BASIC BOOGUMS...

PPHPHPT!!

YEEOW!

PORTRAIT.. OF AN ANXIETY ATTACK.

YES YOU WERE!!... YOU WERE ADOPTED FROM KURDISH YAK HERDERS!! IT'S TRUE!

NO IT ISN'T! NO IT ISN'T!!

89

EXCUSE US, SIR...BUT WHAT--?

SSHH! I'M KEEPING AN EYE ON ONE OF MY BIGGEST ANXIETIES.

WHICH ONE IS THAT?

THAT ONE THERE... THE ONE LURKING IN THE SHADOWS... "IMPENDING PUBERTY."

NOT A SIGHT FOR THE FAINT OF HEART NOR THE HAIRLESS OF CHEST.

THEY SAY THAT ONE'S CAPACITY FOR LOGIC AND REASON COMES FROM THE LEFT SIDE OF THE BRAIN...

AND THAT ONE'S POTENTIAL FOR EMOTIONS AND FEELINGS COME FROM THE RIGHT SIDE.

NOW, CONSIDERING MY OWN MARKEDLY LOPSIDED PERSONALITY...

..I'M SURPRISED I JUST DON'T GO FLOPPIN' OVER TO THE RIGHT FROM ALL THE WEIGHT.

SO, WHADDYA SAY WE MELT ON OVER TO MY PLACE FOR A LITTLE OF THE OL' KOOTCHIE-KOO SKIDDOO?

UH...

GREAT, BABY. BUT FIRST I'D APPRECIATE YOU SIGNING THIS PRE-AFFAIR CONTRACT.

BESIDES ABSOLVING ME OF ALL EMOTIONAL COMMITMENT, IT MAKES YOU LIABLE FOR BROKEN FURNITURE, TORN CLOTHING, 1/2 THE COST OF MEALS AND ALL CAR REPAIRS WHEN YOU ROAR OFF IN A JEALOUS RAGE AND WRAP MY NEW CAMARO AROUND A TELEPHONE POLE.

DOES IT MAKE ME LIABLE FOR DENTAL WORK AFTER I KICK YOUR TEETH IN?

NO, BUT NOTE THE HERPES CLAUSE, HERE...

GOOD HEAVENS! STEVE! WHAT HAPPENED TO YOU? DON'T TELL ME! ANOTHER WOMAN KICKED YOU IN THE TEETH FOR BEING A TWIT! OH, MY! DON'T MOVE! OH, MY!

A DOCTOR!! IS THERE A DOCTOR IN THE HOUSE?! IS...UH..WAIT..

A GOOD PLASTIC SURGEON! IS THERE A GOOD PLASTIC SURGEON IN THE HOUSE?!

MY NOTHE.. DAMMIT, WHERE 'TH MY NOTHE?

IF YOU PROMISE NOT TO TAKE ANY OF THIS PERSONALLY, I'LL READ YOU YOUR STANDING IN THE POLLS THIS MORNING...

GRUNT.

LESSEE...A "MINUS 17%." IN FACT, THEY SAY THAT FOR V.P., THE ONLY THING THAT THE AMERICAN PEOPLE WOULD PREFER LESS THAN YOURSELF IS... IS... UH...OH, DEAR...

SLURP.

...A CUCUMBER.

PPHWEPTH!

WOULD THEY HAVE TOLD LINCOLN AT 5:38 a.m. THAT HE WAS BARELY AHEAD OF A CUCUMBER IN THE POLLS? NO. ROOSEVELT? NO. TRUMAN? NO. CARTER? POSSIBLY BUT NOT NECESSARILY.

THAT'S IT. WE'RE STALLED. THE MEADOW CANDIDATES ARE RUNNING −23% IN THE POLLS. WHAT THIS CAMPAIGN NEEDS IS AN ELECTRIFYING POLITICAL WINDFALL STRAIGHT FROM HEAVEN...

PHWUMP!

POING!

The Bloom Beacon

JACKSONS COMING TO TOWN—WOW!

"A GREAT POLITICAL WINDFALL FOR SOMEBODY," SAYS EXPERT

"MICHAEL IS NICE," SAYS NANCY REAGA... "BUT MY FAVE-RAVE... WALLY CLEAVER"

92

UH... A MISTER OPUS TO SEE MISTER MICHAEL JACKSON, PLEASE.

RIGHT. AND I'M KOJAK.

YOU CRAZY KIDS... ALWAYS TRYIN' TO SNOWBALL YOUR WAY PAST-- SON OF A GUN... HERE'S YER NAME!

COME IN, CENTRAL. THIS IS "RED LEADER." GOT SOMEONE HERE TO SEE "PETER PAN ONE." SEND OVER "GOOD FAIRY SIX" FOR ESCORT.

WHO?

WIPE YOUR FEET AND FOLLOW ME, PLEASE.

WELCOME, MR. OPUS. I'M MICHAEL'S PERSONAL APPOINTMENTS FAIRY. PLEASE FOLLOW ME TO HIS SUITE.

WHO ARE ALL THESE OTHER PEOPLE?

HIS TOUR ENTOURAGE. SERVANTS... SYCOPHANTS... ASSORTED BROTHERS... AH... AND HERE'S MR. FERN, MICHAEL'S NEW PERSONAL ASSISTANT!

OH, DEAR... MICHAEL STILL ISN'T EATING HIS SOY BEAN LASAGNA, MR. FERN?

NO. OR THE BRAN MUFFINS. OR THE BANANA ENCHILADAS. AND I'M GETTIN' SICK OF THIS STUPID GET-UP!

MR. FERN HASN'T QUITE GOTTEN INTO THE RHYTHM OF OUR LITTLE FAMILY YET.

SAY, LET'S JUST THROW "HAPPY FEET" BACK THERE OUT A WINDOW AND GO HOME.

HERE WE ARE, MR. OPUS. "MR. TIN SOLDIER" WILL SHOW YOU IN TO MICHAEL.

BEEP!

"GOOD FAIRY SIX" HERE. UH-HUH... IS HER NAME ON THE LIST? UH-HUH... AND SHE STILL WON'T LEAVE? RIGHT. OKAY... I'LL COME DOWN.

PLEASE EXCUSE ME... THERE'S A LITTLE TROUBLE AT THE SOUTH BARRICADE.

BUT I'M HIS MOTHER!

LADY, I WOULDN'T CARE IF YOU WERE HIS ACCOUNTANT... HE'S SEEIN' NOBODY!

93

KNOCK! KNOCK! KNOCK!

♪ TOOT TOOT! TOOT TOOTIE TOOT TOOT! ♪

ANNOUNCING A VISITOR TO THE MAGIC KINGDOM!

E.T.!

NO! NO! DON'T PICK ME UP!

MR. JACKSON? MICHAEL? ARE YOU HERE?

HERE... I AM UP HERE...

OH, YES... THERE YOU ARE UP ON THE SHELF... WITH YOUR SLEEPING BAG.

I FEEL... SAFER UP HERE.

I KNOW WHAT YOU MEAN. YES... I CAN BARELY SEE YOU WITH ALL THE GLARE FROM THE... UH...

SPARKLING. I'M SORRY.

SAY, IS THAT **YOU** GLOWING?

RED ALERT! RED ALERT! "PETER PAN ONE" HAS FLOWN THE COOP!

YES! THAT AWFUL LITTLE MR. OPUS MUST HAVE DRAGGED HIM OUTSIDE! CAN YOU IMAGINE?!

MICHAEL'S GONE?

LARRY! GET THE COPS!... CALL DON KING AND BREAK OUT THE DOGS!

~LOOSE AND UNPROTECTED IN THE COMMON, SAVAGE STREETS!

HIT IT? WHAT... FOR?

WELL, ACTUALLY, THAT'S A GOOD QUESTION...

ATTENTION ASSORTED HOUSEMATES! I AM HOME NOW AND PLAN TO WATCH THE *CUBS* GAME THAT I RECORDED LAST NIGHT ON MY NEW VCR... WHICH, BY THE WAY, I HOPE NOBODY HAS MESSED WITH DURING THE DAY!

=CLICK!=

REWIND
REWIND
REWIND
REWIND
REWIND
REWIND

I KILL WHEN PEOPLE RECORD OVER MY PROGRAMS.

AND NOW... MUTUAL OF OMAHA PRESENTS "PENGUINS: ANTARCTICA'S LITTLE CLOWNS."

MILO... I'M FEELING VERY, *VERY* SMALL, MILO.

SMALL?

YES. A SPECK IN THE UNIVERSE...INSIGNIFICANT. SMALL...TINY... MICROSCOPIC.

LISTEN... COME OVER HERE AND STOMP ON THIS LITTLE BUG.

WHACK!

THERE. YOU'RE HUGE.

MILO... I'M FEELING VERY, *VERY* GUILTY, MILO...

YOU'RE GOING *WHERE?!* TO DO *WHAT?!*

ATLANTIC CITY. TO BE IN THE "MISTER AMERICA PAGEANT." I'M "MISTER BLOOM COUNTY," REMEMBER?

"MISTER BLOO-"? THERE AIN'T NO SUCH THING!

WELL IF THERE WAS, I'D BE IT.

STEVE! THE MISTER AMERICA PAGEANT IS A *CULTURAL DINOSAUR!* IT PERPETUATES A SUPERFICIAL AND SILLY MASCULINE STEREOTYPE!

IT'S ALSO A SPRINGBOARD TO A FAB- ULOUS NEW CAREER.

WHAT *COULD* POSSIBLY BE MORE FABULOUS THAN BEING A LAWYER?!

"THE LOVE BOAT," HERE I COME!

VROOM!!

BACKSTAGE IN ATLANTIC CITY... WITH THE FABULOUS "MISTER AMERICA PAGEANT" ONLY HOURS AWAY, THE EXCITED CONTESTANTS JOKE AND GIGGLE NERVOUSLY AS THEY ALL AWAIT THE CROWNING OF AMERICA'S NEW MANLY IDEAL!

...SO THE NUN SAID, "PASS ME THE AVOCADO!"

HA! HA! HA! HA!

HOOT! HOOT! YOW!

I'M JUST *SO* NERVOUS... SAY, WHAT'RE YOU GONNA DO FOR THE TALENT COMPETITION?

DRINK FOUR SIX-PACKS AND SING 76 VERSES OF "LOUIE, LOUIE" WITHOUT PASSING OUT ONCE.

NOT ONCE?

...OR THROWING UP.

WELL THAT BEATS MY TARGET SPITTING.

I HEAR "MISTER NEW JERSEY" IS BREAKBELCHING.

★Mister Amer

PSSST! STEVE! WATCH YER POSTURE!

WHA-? JEEZ! GET OFF THE STAGE, BLOB!

LOOK AT YOURSELF! YER LOSING POINTS IN THE SWIMSUIT COMPETITION!... FAT GUT...MINUS FOUR POINTS! ITTY-BITTY THIGH PIMPLES... *SIX* POINTS.

OH, BUT THEN DON'T FOR A *SECOND* THINK THAT I BELIEVE THESE AFFAIRS TO BE JUDGED PRIMARILY ON PHYSICAL PERFECTION... OH! HOW TACKY! HOW PERFECTLY *RUDE*!

BUG *OFF*!

DIDN'T I *TELL* YOU TO SHAVE YOUR BACK?! 300 POINTS!!

Amer

PSST! STEVE! SOMETHING IS ROTTEN IN DENMARK!

OR MAYBE I SHOULD SAY IT'S ROTTEN RIGHT HERE ON THIS STAGE. OVER *THERE* TO BE PRECISE ...

...IN FACT, A CERTAIN UNNAMED CONTESTANT APPEARS TO HAVE A MORE...SHALL WE SAY... PRONOUNCED HINEY THAN NATURE ORIGINALLY PROVIDED. BUT FAR BE IT FOR *ME* TO SPREAD VULGAR, TACKY, NAY, *MALICIOUS* RUMOR.

GOOD! NOW GET--

"MISTER RHODE ISLAND" HAS *STUFFED* HIS SUIT!!

100

Panel 1: ≶TAP! TAP!≶ ENTER NEW RECORD: "HOWARD L. JONES, AGE 36. HEIGHT 6 FT. RACE...BLACK. SOC. SEC. # 003-15-9003... SERIAL # 66-77-1140... LICENSE # 3476140... DUCK-HUNTING PERMIT # 78103.

Panel 2: ≶BEEP≶ ≶POOF!≶ ——THIS SORT OF COMPUTER MISCHIEF!

Panel 3: AND FURTHERMORE, I'VE RECENTLY DECIDED THAT IT'S TIME YOU GOT INVOLVED IN SOMETHING MORE NORMAL THAN COMPUTERS! WOULD YOU LIKE TO KNOW WHAT IT IS? WELL I'LL TELL YA...

Panel 4: ≶BEEP!≶ FOOTBALL! BLIP!

Panel 5: TONIGHT ON **NOVA**... "COCKROACHES: AMERICA'S LITTLE HOUSEGUESTS."

Panel 6: THE AMERICAN COCKROACH IS A SHAMELESS LITTLE CREATURE, DISTINGUISHED NOT ONLY BY HIS BRAZEN AND OBNOXIOUS EATING HABITS... MUNCH! MUNCH! PASS THE FRITOS.

Panel 7: ...BUT ALSO BY THE ALARMING BAD TASTE SHOWN IN HIS CHOICE OF TELEVISION ENTERTAINMENT. SWITCH IT, LARRY.

Panel 8: ≶CLICK≶ ...NEXT ON **HBO**... DON KNOTTS SCARES UP SOME LAUGHS IN "THE GHOST AND MR. CHICKEN"! OH, MY CUP RUNNETH OVER.

Panel 9: GOOD EVENING. THIS IS "EYEWITNESS NEWS".

Panel 10: FACED WITH A SKYROCKETING POPULATION OF ROAMING, RAVENOUS "MINI-CAM" NEWS CREWS TRYING TO FEED OFF TOO LITTLE NEWS, THE DEPT. OF THE INTERIOR TODAY ANNOUNCED A "THINNING" PROGRAM.

Panel 11: STARTING TONIGHT, ANY "MINI-CAM" CREWS FOUND LOOSE WILL BE CLUBBED, SKINNED AND THEIR INTERNAL ORGANS SOLD AS APHRODISIACS IN CHINA.

Panel 12: YOU'LL UNDERSTAND IF WE WON'T BE BRINGING YOU ANY FILM OF THE HUNT... OH, ABSOLUTELY!

TODAY, THE GOVERNMENT-SUBSIDIZED "MINI-CAM" SLAUGHTER CONTINUES UNABATED.

ZZ... SNORT.

ENTIRE HERDS OF NEWS CREWS ARE BEING PREYED UPON AS THEY FLOUNDER HELPLESSLY, LOOKING FOR STORIES IN TRAGICALLY OVERGRAZED AREAS SUCH AS BEACHES AND PARKS ...

OUR OWN REPORTER, DOT KERNS, WAS SPOTTED BY HUNTERS AS SHE WRAPPED UP A FILM REPORT ON "LULU: THE FRISBEE-CATCHING GRIZZLY" WITH THE SENTENCE, "LIFE WITHOUT LULU WOULD TRULY BE...UN**BEAR**ABLE!"

SHE WAS IMMEDIATELY CLUBBED AND SKINNED.

ZZ... SNORT...

H.. HELLO? ≥COUGH!≤ IS...IS ANYBODY THERE...? ≥COUGH!≤ THIS...IS...JEFF GREENBLATT... REPORTING FOR... ≥COUGH!≤ EYEWITNESS NEWS...

I'M...I'M THE LAST SURVIVOR... ≥COUGH!≤ THEY...FOUND ME FILMING A STORY ON "WHEEL-CHAIR MIMES"... ≥COUGH!≤ THEY CUT OFF MY EARS AND SET MY HAIRPIECE ON FIRE... ≥COUGH!≤

EVERYONE...ELSE... ≥COUGH!≤ GONE...DEAD...CARCASSES EVERYWHERE... ≥GAG!≤ THE...THE ONCE-MIGHTY HERDS OF MEDIA... ≥COUGH!≤ ARE WIPED OUT! ≥ EXTINCT!

THIS MORNING, "GREENPEACE" RELEASED A STATEMENT OF GENERAL APPROVAL.

GOOD EVENING. PLEASE MEET—IF YOU HAVEN'T ALREADY—MY ANXIETY CLOSET.

KNOCK! KNOCK!

...AN ENCLOSURE OF CHILDISH BEASTIES AND ASSORTED BOOGUMS...ALL OF WHICH I'VE LONG AGO LEARNED TO DEAL WITH RATIONALLY.

KNOCK! KNOCK!

WHO IIIIIIIS IT?

JUST ME! YOUR MORTALITY!

YA'LL EXCUSE ME WHILE I CRAWL UNDER THE FLOOR-BOARDS ...

CAN WE TALK?

106

"CHOCOLATE ECLAIR"

WHAT?

YOU WANTED TO KNOW WHAT SORT OF IMAGE TODAY'S VOTERS ARE MOST WANTING TO FIND IN A PRESIDENTIAL CANDIDATE.

SO?

SO THE COMPUTER SAYS "CHOCOLATE ECLAIR".

THAT'S LUDICROUS.

NO, JUST SILLY. "PEANUT FARMER" WAS LUDICROUS.

MILO! I'VE MADE A TERRIBLE MISTAKE! I MUST HAVE MIXED UP MY MOTHER'S PASTRY RECIPE FILES WITH MY POLLING RESULTS!!

I'M AFRAID THAT THE AMERICAN VOTER HASN'T EVEN THE FAINTEST DESIRE FOR A PRESIDENTIAL CANDIDATE WITH A "CHOCOLATE ECLAIR" IMAGE!

OH DEAR. I'VE CAUSED SOME PROBLEMS, HAVEN'T I? WHERE'S OPUS?

WORKING THE WEST SIDE.

GREETINGS!

UP EARLY FOR SOME LAST MINUTE CAMPAIGNING, EH? HA! GO BACK TO BED!

BRUSH BRUSH BRUSH

LISTEN TO ME, YOUR BETTER INSTINCTS. YOU'RE NOT CUT FROM VICE PRESIDENTIAL TIMBER! YOU'RE A GOOF! KNOW YOUR LIMITATIONS! TAKE AN HONEST LOOK AT YOURSELF!

THAT'S RIGHT. LOOK LONG AND DEEP... WHAT DO YOU SEE?

I SEE THAT I'VE BRUSHED MY TEETH WITH "PREPARATION 'H'."

RIGHT. GO BACK TO BED.

YOU!! YOU GOT ME INTO THIS RIDICULOUS CAMPAIGN, YOU... YOU STUPID MOO!!

WELL, NO MORE POLITICS! ..NO MORE POLLS! ..NO MORE DEBATES! NEVER!!

CHUNK!

LISTEN..YOU'RE DISTRAUGHT... MONDALE IS TOO! CAN I SAY JUST ONE WORD? JUST ONE...

NO! I'M NOT LISTENING! PHPTFPH! PPHTPH!

..."1988."

HEY... WHOA... YEAH!

A NIGHTMARE, DAD. I'VE HAD A HORRIBLE NIGHTMARE.

I DREAMT I CAME IN HERE IN THE MIDDLE OF THE NIGHT TO DISCUSS CELEBRITY GOSSIP... AND THEN AS USUAL, YOU RUDELY TOLD ME TO BUG OFF.... AND THEN I WENT TO THE KITCHEN FOR A MEAT CLEAVER, CAME BACK AND DISMEMBERED YOU IN YOUR SLEEP.

SHOCKING. THE WHOLE THING. SHOCKING.

...BUT THEN NO MORE SO THAN THE RECENT DIVORCE OF JOHN AND CHRISTINA DELOREAN. WHAT DO YOU THINK?

HAVE A SEAT! WE'LL DISCUSS IT!

NO, I DO NOT THINK WE SHOULD LET BILL THE CAT "ROT WITH THE RAJNEESHEES". I THINK WE SHOULD RESCUE THE LITTLE FELLOW...

Spec HAM #2

JUST IMAGINE HIM RIGHT NOW...SITTING AROUND IN A PINK TUNIC...BRAINWASHED... CHANTING INCOMPREHENSIBLY...

EATING SOY CAKES... WEAVING RUGS...

..WRITING CHECKS TO THE "BHAGWAN" FROM OUR CAMPAIGN FUND...

BY GOD, WE'VE GOT TO RESCUE THAT POOR BOY.

SAY, BROTHER...UH, HOW ABOUT REFRESHING ME ON THIS RAJNEESH BUSINESS...

HAPPY PEAS

WELL, RAJNEESH IS THE TRUTH.. AND THE TRUTH IS THE LIGHT.. WHICH IS LIFE. LIFE'S TRUTH LIGHT. AND HAPPINESS. WHICH IS WEARING RED PAJAMAS AND BLOWING KISSES TOWARD THE BHAGWAN'S 72 GOLD ROLLS-ROYCES.

WHOA! BY GOLLY...THAT DOES MAKE A LOT OF SENS--

PSST! OPUS! SNAP OUT OF IT!!

PANT! PANT! WELL YOU HAVE TO ADMIT... PANT! PANT! THAT'S A FRIGHTENINGLY SEDUCTIVE PHILOSOPHY!!

SAY... AREN'T YOU ANNE BURFORD?

I USED TO BE, BROTHER. NOW I'M "RAJNOOSH SWANI GORSEESH".

AND THEY USED TO BE JAMES WATT, RICHARD ALLEN, RITA LAVELLE AND RAY DONOVAN!...

...LOST SHEEP, EVERY ONE... FORCED OUT OF THE FLOCK AND LEFT TO WANDER A COLD, SUSPICIOUS, LIBERAL WORLD... SHUNNED LIKE LEPERS... UNTIL NOW.

WELL, I'M GLAD YOU ALL HAVE FINALLY FOUND YOUR PLACE!

YES, YOU KNOW WE'RE SAVING A COT FOR ED MEESE ...

THE CABIN OF BHAGWAN BILL

NO CHANTING

OOF! GRUNT! OUCH!

THE CABIN OF BHAGWAN BILL

NO CHANTING

ACKMMPH!

START THE CAR!!

MILO JUST CALLED. THEY GOT BILL THE CAT...

...BUT UNFORTUNATELY HE'S SHOWN A LITTLE RESISTANCE TO COMING HOME...

APPARENTLY IT'S BEEN THE CAUSE OF SOME MINOR PROBLEMS...

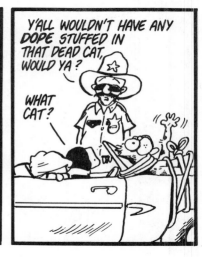
Y'ALL WOULDN'T HAVE ANY DOPE STUFFED IN THAT DEAD CAT, WOULD YA?

WHAT CAT?

BILL'S BACK. THEY'VE GOT HIM TIED UP IN MILO'S ATTIC.

BILL? HE'S BACK?

DID YOU SEE HIM? HOW WAS HE? IS HE THE SAME OLD BILL THE CAT THAT WE KNOW AND LOATHE?!

GREAT SCOTT, MAN... HE ISN'T ANY DIFFERENT, IS HE? HOW DOES HE LOOK??

EMBALMED.

OH, THANK THE GODS.

"DEPROGRAMMING" A CULT VICTIM LIKE BILL IS A NASTY BUSINESS, BINKLEY. NO MATTER WHAT YOU HEAR, DO NOT ENTER THE ATTIC.

HOW LONG WILL IT TAKE?

HOURS. DAYS. MONTHS. ALL I KNOW IS THAT OUR PRESIDENTIAL CANDIDATE NEEDS TO BE DRAGGED BACK INTO THE REAL WORLD!

HURT HIM WITH LOVE, MILO!

-WITH LOVE!

HE'S OFF!

FORGOT MY BULLWHIP.